REIMAGINE
Home

Devotions, Recipes, and Tips
for Loving Your Home Through Every Season

SARABETH GALIMBA

Ink &
Willow

*To my husband, Jeremy, for being my biggest
supporter and for making my dreams come true.
To my children, Jaden, Logan, Maddie, and Abbie—
may the wisdom in this devotional be something you
experience in your own homes one day.*

Contents

A Time for Everything 8

Fall

Winter

A TIME
for Everything

For everything there is a season,
a time for every activity under heaven.

—ECCLESIASTES 3:1 (NLT)

WITH EACH PASSING YEAR, I have gained a greater understanding of the truth that life is meant to be experienced in seasons. Whether we like it or not, our lives are seasonal, with times to reset, times to celebrate, times to gather, and times to rest. Though each season is drastically different from the others, it is also uniquely valuable and necessary. Seasons are also part of God's creative design, not just for the planet Earth but also for the places we call home.

Whenever we direct ourselves or our expectations away from God's design, the misalignment brings unnecessary stress and complexity into our lives. Fortunately, the opposite is also true. If we intentionally align ourselves with how God has designed the world, we are able to experience refreshing simplicity in our lives. This simple and seasonal perspective on life can be so transformative, particularly when it comes to our homes.

In today's society, it is so easy to be overwhelmed by an unhealthy pressure to have our homes looking like the latest magazine photo or Instagram post. As a result, we can find ourselves always searching for more luxury and perfection, instead of stewarding our homes towards hospitality and simplicity.

Whether you live in an apartment, condo, townhouse, camper van, two-story house, mansion, or anything in between, may this book invite you into seeing your home for the gift it is. As you read through the devotions, may you become grounded in the natural rhythms of life that God has created, and may the practical tips offered here encourage you to seek the beauty of simplicity that can be found in every season.

How to Use This Book

This book is equal parts devotional and practical guide. Depending on your current season, you can choose to focus more on the reflections or skip those for now in favor of the home styling tips included at the end of each section. You can also read everything in order or jump around as you prefer. Just as every home is unique and different, your experience with this book can be as individualized and personalized as you would like it to be.

The bite-sized inspirational essays are meant to offer you little moments of encouragement, peace, and calm in an otherwise busy or full day, whether you're running around your house all day managing chaos or whether you only arrive home in time to collapse into bed. These short reflections on life, home, and scripture invite you into a comforting space where you can pause, breathe, and rest in God's loving presence.

At the close of each reflection, you will find a Reimagine section that includes a few questions to prompt further exploration or application of the theme from that reflection. These questions will help you align your thinking with what God says about you and your home. Feel free to think about your responses, write them down in a journal, or discuss them with a friend or family member.

In addition to the Reimagine section, each reflection also includes a Refresh section with practical tips, simple decor ideas, delicious recipes, or fun activities for you to try out while navigating each season in your home. As you experiment with applying these refreshes to your home and its routine, feel free to tweak some of the steps or come up with your own ideas. After all, you're the best expert on your own home! These tips are merely meant to inspire you in creating your own rhythms, traditions, styles, and dreams for the home God has given you.

SPRING

A Time to Reset

Therefore, if anyone is in Christ,
he is a new creation.
The old has passed away; behold,
the new has come.

−2 CORINTHIANS 5:17 (ESV)

LAUNCHING A RESET is always one of the first steps we try when our tech devices are not working properly. The same can be said for most things. Just about everything around us needs a time to reset, including our homes. In the natural world, spring functions as the season for resetting. Whether with freshly formed flowers or newly born babies, the end of winter is always met by a chance to restart and grow again.

Resetting usually requires a willingness to let go of the old in order to look toward something new. In his second letter to the Corinthian church, the apostle Paul wrote that part of being a new creation in Christ means that the old needs to pass away. An easy enough statement to say, but it can be really hard to put into practice. Sometimes we like "the good old stuff," and exchanging it for the new can feel scary or uncomfortable. But change—like in the seasons—is a natural part of life, and the act of surrendering can often lead to beautiful results.

During this spring season of resetting, don't be afraid to let go of some old things or thoughts that may be keeping you from pursuing a better way forward, whether those are physical items cluttering your home or unhealthy habits keeping you from embracing and expressing the values you want to cultivate. As you explore the elements of the spring season, let the small changes you make in your home inspire you to allow resets in other areas of your life. Keep it simple, stay committed to the growing process, and remember that resetting opens the doors for new life, new opportunities, and new growth—and occasionally a Wi-Fi router that works.

Reimagine

When have you experienced
a positive form of reset
in your life?

Which specific area of
your home is most in need
of a reset right now?

Where could you use a reset in
your life currently?

Resetting a Room
A Fresh Look

Spring is a perfect time for a reset, not only when it comes to creating new goals for the year, but also when it comes to refreshing our homes. After months of looking at the same decor or navigating around the same arrangement of furniture, spring offers us the option of a new perspective and maybe even a new aesthetic.

Keep in mind you don't have to completely redecorate or remodel during this season to experience a refresh. Sometimes all you need is to switch out some decorative items or shift a piece of furniture. If buying any new pieces, be sure to review your finances carefully and decide *beforehand* how much you are willing and able to spend. If your budget is limited, remember that thrift stores, secondhand shops, and online marketplaces are great resources. After all, what doesn't fit in someone else's home might be new and exciting for your space!

Tips for Refreshing a Room

- Change up the wall decor by spray painting your picture frames, finding affordable prints, or creating your own artwork. Feel free to store, sell, or donate your existing decor depending on whether you think you or someone else might use it in the future.

- Decorate with meaning and purpose by framing family photos or art pieces that are significant to you. If someone in the house is a photographer or artist, display their art!

- Add mirrors to the end of a hallway, across from a window, in the entryway, or in other "nook and cranny" places to help make a room feel wider and more open (thrift or antique shops usually have cheap options!).

- Shift the furniture to make the most of your space and the natural light from windows.

- Switch out curtains to change the feel of a room, being mindful of the current season.

- Update pillows, pillow shams, towels, linens, or throw blankets. Try to use lighter colors and fabrics for spring and summer.

- Make the most of an area rug by choosing one with lots of colors and then "pulling out" a different color during different seasons with other decorative pieces (e.g., throw blankets, pillows, candles, wall art, etc.).

- Minimize clutter by maximizing how you decorate. Instead of having random knick-knacks, try to incorporate items you use into a room's decor, such as books, lamps, vases, candles, plants, or a bowl of real fruit.

TASKS

Stewardship

Then he said, "Beware! Guard against every kind of greed. Life is not measured by how much you own."

—LUKE 12:15 (NLT)

I CAN CLEARLY remember the day when I stood in our guest bedroom closet feeling completely overwhelmed, looking at all the stuff we had collected over the years. Packed from ceiling to floor with home decor for every season, that closet had enabled me to hoard more things than I was ever meant to possess.

We all have that place in our homes where we put all the random stuff we collect. For a few of us it manages to take up only a drawer, for some of us it fits in a closet, and for others it requires a whole room. It's a struggle we all have, and it all centers around stewardship. How content are we with the possessions God has shared with us?

In one of his parables, Jesus told a story about a rich man who had an abundance of possessions, to the point where it filled up all of his barns. Instead of being content and grateful with what he had, he chose to tear down his barns and build bigger ones just so he wouldn't have to get rid of anything. Through this parable, Jesus reminds us that our lives are not measured by how much we own. He also told us to be on guard because greediness can show up in a lot of different ways. And for me, that was definitely in my collection of home decor.

Where do you keep accumulating more and more stuff? Is it in your shoe closet, kitchen cabinets, or garage? Wherever it may be, try to take a step back this week and really evaluate those items from a future-minded perspective. Have they blessed others? Do they bring joy to you because of what they are or because of the status they bring you? As you consider ways you might minimize in your home, keep in mind Jesus's words about what actually brings worth to our lives.

Reimagine

What is one way you are positively stewarding your home or possessions?

What is something you feel you could let go of this season?

How could you be a better steward of what God has given you?

Spring Cleaning

Declutter Matrix

The French have two rules for meal preparation that relate perfectly to home design. The first is *mise-en-scène*, which literally means to "set the stage." When getting your home ready for the spring, it is important to decide what belongs on "the stage" and what you should let go. Your home should be a place for staging, not for storing.

The second rule is *mise en place*, which means to "put in place." In our home, we often repeat the common phrase "a place for everything, and everything in its place." Once you have decided what belongs on the stage of your home, you need to make sure that it has a place to be stored when not in use. From cutlery to candles, or paintings to pillow shams, everything that you use needs its own place to call home. I personally prefer to organize all my furnishings in labeled plastic tubs, which I end up storing in my attic. That way it is much easier for me to make quick seasonal shifts in my home without needing to dig through piles of decor. Setting your stage and putting everything in its place are the two easiest ways to keep your home feeling fresh and ready for something new.

Whatever your home collection "guilty pleasure" might be, one way to keep yourself in check is to have an annual spring-cleaning routine in order to maintain a decluttered and simplified home. Whether in spring or during any other time of the year, this handy little chart can help you better steward what God has shared with you.

Choose one room or space in your home on which to apply the Declutter Matrix on the opposite page.

Stage *it*

These refer to items that you are planning to use in your room right away. They are items of either high value, personal sentimentality, or good quality that can be used for many years to come.

Store *it*

These include items that you plan to use in the future. They are items of high value and quality that are worth saving. Just make sure you have enough space.

Share *it*

These are items that you may have enjoyed over the years but are not currently using. They are quality items that someone you know might enjoy for years to come.

Sell *it*

These include items that are not worth keeping. They are valuable enough to sell, or you can simply donate these items to a local nonprofit enterprise.

TRADITIONS
Good Ground

And the seeds that fell on the good soil represent honest,
good-hearted people who hear God's word, cling to it,
and patiently produce a huge harvest.

—LUKE 8:15 (NLT)

WHEN IT COMES TO GARDENING, I always seem to have more black thumb moments than green ones. Growing up watching my grandma grow just about anything she ever planted, I assumed creating my own garden would be just as easy.

Well, needless to say, my expectations were a little too high for my first round. Whether it was our finicky fiddle-leaf figs or short-lived succulents, I became quite frustrated when I didn't immediately see the luscious garden I had dreamed of.

One spring season, I was sharing my garden woes with a farming family member when he said, "The only thing you really need is better soil." He went on to ask a farmer friend if I could have a little bit of soil from his local field. After using that rich soil in our garden, I have been amazed at the results we've seen. Just a little change in soil, and the results were incredible.

We often underestimate the power that soil has when it comes to healthy growth. The old saying is certainly true: a plant's fruit will only be as healthy as its root. And a plant's root will only be as healthy as its soil. This is true not only for plants but also for our own spiritual lives and for the physical homes we curate to live in.

Jesus alluded to this principle in Luke 8, when he compared people to soil and his Word to seed. Read the whole chapter for yourself, and when you do, try to reflect on your relationship with God's Word and how much (or little) you allow it to enrich the garden of your soul. What traditions have you cultivated in your spiritual life? Do you have a daily or weekly habit of digging into Scripture?

Reimagine

What is one simple action step
you can take this week to help
you grow spiritually?

Where in your home can
you dedicate a "sacred space" for you
to be alone with God?

Classic Compost

The Easiest Compost Ever

Composting can feel like an overwhelming task, but once you set up a basic system, it's actually quite manageable. And since part of God's purpose for us is to care for the earth, composting is an important way we can steward the gift of creation. Of course, not all of us have access to yards where we can start cultivating a compost pile, but additional options exist. If you live in an apartment or a more urban area, you might look into getting a compost bin, scheduling compost pickup, or finding a community or shared compost situation. If you do have your own yard space, see the instructions below.

Greens	Browns
fruit and vegetable peels	leaves
grass clippings	hay and straw
coffee grounds	sawdust
manure (from herbivores only)	eggshells
plant cuttings	tea bags
weeds	paper
any other food scraps or biodegradable items from the kitchen (avoid meat)	cardboard

Find a space in the garden where you can make a heap—on soil rather than paving if possible. Or you could buy a ready-made composting bin.

Whenever you have any garden waste or uncooked kitchen waste, throw it on top. Make sure there is always a good mixture of greens and browns.

Check occasionally to make sure it's not too wet or dry. It should be damp but not dripping. If it's too wet, fork in some dry browns; if it's too dry, add some water.

After about six months, the pile should have rotted down to a brown crumbly mixture that can be added to the soil in the garden. If it isn't rotting down, it may need more air; try poking and lifting the compost with a garden fork to introduce oxygen into the mix.

TASTES
Diligence

The plans of the diligent lead to profit
as surely as haste leads to poverty.

—PROVERBS 21:5

NOTHING AWAKENS MY TASTEBUDS to the spring season quite like biting into a freshly picked strawberry! Because I grew up in an agricultural community, I have many memories of driving by the fields and watching workers earnestly harvesting ripe strawberries. My grandparents would also tell me stories of how they picked strawberries in the field for hours on end, and I couldn't help but admire their hard work and diligence.

It is a simple truth, but so many things we enjoy or admire in life are only a product of hard work. Whether it is picking strawberries, preparing a meal, planning an event, or parenting children, just about everything we do has some element of diligence involved in it. Unfortunately, diligence is never the easiest and fastest way to do things. However, it is the only pathway that leads to meaningful accomplishment. The good news is that we were all made to do difficult things. So don't let fear, exhaustion, or even boredom cause you to give up too easily, when all you need to do is stick with it a little longer.

In what areas of your life do you tend to be hasty and impatient? In which spaces are you tempted to take the reins from God and act rashly instead of waiting and trusting in his timing? On the other hand, can you think of a time when you worked hard or diligently at something and produced a satisfying result?

Reimagine

Which activities, tasks,
or chores tend to make you
feel the most impatient?

What is one way you can
practice a posture of faithful
diligence this week?

Fruit Tart

Practicing Diligence

Though it definitely requires some diligence in preparation, this fruit tart is a light and colorful way to celebrate the flavors of spring, as well as a fun way to highlight all of the hard work that goes into producing the fresh fruits of the season.

MAKES ONE
9-inch tart

Pastry Cream

1½ cups whole milk

½ cup heavy cream

½ cup sugar

Pinch of salt

3 tablespoons cornstarch

5 egg yolks

4 tablespoons cold unsalted butter, cut into chunks

1½ teaspoons vanilla extract

Pastry Cream

In a medium saucepan over medium-high heat, combine the milk, cream, and half of the sugar, stirring occasionally until the liquid comes to a simmer.

As the liquid heats, in a medium bowl whisk together the remaining sugar, salt, cornstarch, and egg yolks until light and creamy.

Once the milk mixture is hot, slowly whisk about 1 cup of the liquid into the egg mixture to temper the yolks. Pour the tempered egg mixture into the saucepan with the hot milk mixture and reduce the heat to medium, continuing to cook while whisking constantly, until thickened and a few bubbles burst on the surface, about 30 seconds.

Remove the pastry cream from the heat and whisk in the butter and vanilla, then transfer to a bowl and cover with a sheet of plastic wrap placed directly onto the surface of the pastry cream so a skin does not form. Refrigerate until chilled and firm, about 3 hours.

Recipe continues on next page

Tart Shell

1 egg yolk

1 tablespoon heavy cream

½ teaspoon vanilla extract

1¼ cups all-purpose flour, plus more for the work surface

⅔ cup powdered sugar

¼ teaspoon salt

8 tablespoons cold unsalted butter, cut into chunks

Fruit Topping

(feel free to use the fruits of your choice!)

10 to 12 strawberries, hulled and sliced

4 to 5 nectarines, pitted and sliced

½ cup blueberries, washed

½ cup raspberries, washed

½ cup warmed apple jelly or apricot preserves, for brushing on top

Tart Shell

In a small bowl, whisk together the egg yolk, cream, and vanilla.

In a food processor, combine the flour, powdered sugar, and salt and briefly process to combine. Add the cold butter pieces to the flour mixture and pulse to cut into the flour until the mixture resembles coarse meal, about 15 pulses.

While the food processor is running, add the liquid through the feed tube and continue to process just until the dough comes together around the blade.

Turn out the tart dough onto a sheet of plastic wrap and flatten into a 6-inch disk, then wrap it tightly and refrigerate for 1 hour. Let it sit out on the counter for 10 minutes to soften slightly before rolling out.

Roll out the pastry crust on a lightly floured surface until it is slightly larger than your tart pan (mine is a 9-inch pan). Carefully transfer the dough to the pan by rolling it onto the rolling pin, then gently easing the dough into the pan, pressing into the corners and fluted sides of the pan.

Run the rolling pin over the top of the pan so that the excess dough gets cut off on the edge of the pin, making a clean edge. Patch any edges that are too thin with excess dough, trimming away the edge again as necessary. Freeze the tart shell for 30 minutes.

When ready to bake the tart shell, heat oven to 375°F. Press a double layer of foil into the frozen tart shell, covering the edges of the pan and filling the tart shell with pie weights. Bake for 30 minutes, rotating halfway through, then carefully remove the pie weights and foil and bake another 5 to 10 minutes, until the tart shell is fully baked and golden. Cool completely.

Once the shell is cooled, fill with the pastry cream. Then arrange the strawberries, nectarines, blueberries, and raspberries (or fruit of your choice), starting on the outside and then moving toward the center. Warm the jelly or preserves in the microwave or on low heat on the stove and then brush over the top of the fruit. If the jelly hardens while brushing it on the fruit, feel free to reheat as needed.

SIGHTS

Fruitfulness

I am the vine; you are the branches. If you remain in me and I in you, you will bear much fruit; apart from me you can do nothing.

—JOHN 15:5

NO OTHER SEASON is filled with more life and vibrance than spring. It is a time when everything that was seemingly dead during the winter comes back to life in the blink of an eye. After what has seemed like endless cold, we can finally take hikes along the coastline or in the woods, admire all of the brand-new blossoms covering the trees, and smell the sweet fresh air mingling with the scents of flower buds and mown grass. We can enjoy drives with the windows rolled down and gaze out at the once dull-looking hills that have transformed into a rich green with all the newly sprouted plants.

When we see all this new life springing up around us, we have a perfect picture of the kind of new life that Christ brings. In John 15, Jesus used the metaphor of vines, branches, and bearing fruit to describe the importance of remaining faithful and connected to him in order to experience fruitfulness in our lives. Being in common union with Jesus—in the good, bad, plentiful, and dry times—is the only way we can be fruitful in every season.

Spring Florals

Colors of Spring

When it comes to decorating in the spring, we should try to draw inspiration from the natural world. During this season of new life and fresh growth, a myriad of plants, flowers, and greenery appears in abundance to decorate the earth. In a way, God's natural rhythm for creation is the first and best example of spring remodeling! We can incorporate some of this seasonal miracle into our homes by using fresh flowers or greens in our decor. It's a cheaper way to decorate, and the results can add so much freshness to a space!

- Gather wildflowers or buy flowers from a nearby nursery or farmer's market and arrange them in vases around your home.

- Observe the pops of color that appear naturally in the spring and introduce some of those into your decor.

- Borrow from what you see in nature or from what is currently in season.

- Incorporate fresh scents into your home with flora such as eucalyptus or dried lavender.

- Forage for branches and vines to use as garlands on shelves or mantelpieces. (Greenery doesn't need to be just a filler; it can fill a whole vase!)

- Buy houseplants for the bathrooms. Ficus plants are great options that are easy to maintain.

- If you have time, try creating your own spring wreath for the front door, using store-bought plants or flowers you find in nature.

- Consider fun floral prints for your blankets, pillows, wall art, or wallpaper.

Reimagine

What brings you joy in
the spring season?

How do the themes of
new beginnings and fresh
starts encourage you
during this season?

SOUNDS

Joy

Look at the birds of the air; they do not sow or reap or store away in barns, and yet your heavenly Father feeds them. Are you not much more valuable than they?

—MATTHEW 6:26

ONE OF THE MOST ICONIC sounds of spring has to be the sound of birds singing to each other. We have several large trees around our property that provide the perfect home for a variety of birds to nest in during the spring. I love listening to them chirp to each other in the morning—even if it does provide a bit of an early wake-up call!

Birds make several appearances in the Bible, but one of the most memorable mentions takes place during Jesus's Sermon on the Mount. Picture the scene: Ordinary people from all walks of life—all with their own everyday problems and challenges—gathering to listen to what Jesus had to say. The sheer volume and variety of those all crowded on that hill must have caused a lot of noise, distractions, and commotion. In that setting, Jesus directed everyone's attention to the birds in the sky above them and the flowers below them. Using these elements of nature as examples of how God cares for even the smallest things, Jesus reminds us of an important truth: We are valuable and we are loved, not because of what we do, but because of who we are.

Amid overcrowded schedules, full households, endless to-do lists, and constant anxieties, we can easily lose sight of how valuable we are in the sight of God. But checking off every task and running a perfect home are not prerequisites for God to take delight in us. And our own joy and peace of mind should not be dependent on them either. Rather, the knowledge that the creator of the universe both knows and loves us should be reason enough for us to be joyful in any circumstance.

Reimagine

As you go about your day, take note of the "ordinary" moments that spark a sacred time for you to rejoice over how much God knows and loves you. If you have time, make a list of "small" joys or blessings you encounter.

Creating a Soundtrack
Playlists for the Home

Beyond birdsong, what specific songs or styles of music invite you into a spring mood? What songs or sounds do you typically play as the soundtrack for your home? Which music genres make you feel peaceful, happy, productive, adventurous, motivated, or excited? As you consider your answers to these questions, create your own spring playlist that you can use to fill your heart and home with the refreshing sounds of the season. Feel free to play aloud as you clean, organize, or simply relax in your home. As you listen, remember that no matter what you are worried about, God already knows about it and can provide exactly what you need when you need it.

As a bonus, try creating a specific "home" playlist for every season, mood, or holiday of the year! Below are some possible themes you can use for inspiration:

- Spring
- Summer
- Fall
- Winter
- Road Trip
- Valentine's Day

- Cozy
- Peaceful
- Cooking in the Kitchen
- Thanksgiving
- Christmas

SOCIALS

Surprises

For by grace you have been saved through faith.
And this is not your own doing; it is the gift of God,
not a result of works, so that no one may boast.

—EPHESIANS 2:8-9 (ESV)

ONE OF THE MOST EXCITING and meaningful events of the spring season is the celebration of Easter. On that Sunday, our family enjoys gathering with others to remember the resurrection of Jesus. After sharing a meal together, we prepare a traditional Easter egg hunt for the kids. Before releasing them to run frantically around the yard, the adults strategically hide a few special eggs that contain a surprise gift of money. It is so rewarding to see the faces of the kids when they open up an egg filled with a twenty-dollar bill. At that moment, you can tell the lucky child feels like the richest kid on the planet!

When approaching Easter, this childlike sense of awe and extreme gratitude is exactly the emotion we should all feel, especially when we reflect on the priceless gift that has been given to us through Jesus's sacrifice on the cross. In his letter to the church at Ephesus, Paul describes salvation through the life, death, and resurrection of Jesus as the most incredible gift of grace that we could ever be given. Even beyond Easter, our lives should reflect the joy of those who have received a gift we could never possibly earn ourselves.

Even if you don't decorate for Easter or host a brunch for your family or friends, your home can still reflect the season's gift of hope and new life. Even in small ways, you can reflect the character of Christ in how you orient your home to serve and love others. Maybe that's by having a bowl of chocolates by the front door or a glass of iced tea or lemonade waiting for anyone who stops by. However you choose to approach this season, try to cultivate a perspective of childlike wonder, whether you find the egg with the twenty-dollar bill or not.

Reimagine

What are your thoughts or feelings whenever you approach the Easter season?

What was your most recent memorable encounter with Jesus?

For whatever reason, the unexpected surprise of Easter never gets old for kids. As an adult, how can you experience the joy of gratitude for the miraculous gift of eternal life?

Cascarones

Mexican Easter Eggs

As fun as decorating and hiding Easter eggs can be, knowing what to do with all those boiled eggs can be a challenge! If you're looking for a new egg tradition in your house, try making *cascarones,* confetti-filled Easter eggs that invite kids and adults of all ages into the festivities and also offer more options when it comes to your breakfast egg preparations. Since *cascarones* only require the eggshell, you can pour out the egg contents and save them for scrambled eggs, omelets, frittatas, or as baking ingredients.

2 dozen eggs

6 cups of white or apple
cider vinegar

4 to 8 drops of
food coloring of your choice
(adjust number of drops
depending on how vibrant
you'd like the colors to be)

2 bags of colored
confetti (about 1 pound;
feel free to adjust
depending on how many
eggs you prepare)

Craft glue

4 sheets of colored
tissue paper

Tap each egg on the counter or with a spoon so that a small dent is created. Carefully peel off the section of cracked shell until a small hole (about half a centimeter) is formed. Empty out the yolk and egg white into a bowl and save for future use by covering it and putting it in the fridge.

In a large bowl, mix the vinegar and food coloring and dip the mostly intact eggshells into the mixture until completely covered. Let the shells soak for 3 to 5 minutes, then remove them from the liquid and set aside to dry, preferably overnight.

When the interiors of the eggs are dry, fill them with confetti. Then glue a circular section of colored tissue paper over the hole.

Hand out or hide the finished *cascarones* and have fun chasing one another around the yard and cracking the eggs over one another's heads! (Break eggs outside to simplify clean up!)

SUMMER

A Time to Celebrate

This is the day that the Lord has made;
let us rejoice and be glad in it.

—PSALM 118:24 (ESV)

EVEN IF YOU DON'T LOVE THE HEAT, summer is one of the best times to fully enjoy the beautiful outdoor world. Whether by going to the beach, camping in the forest, road-tripping to new destinations, or simply barbecuing in the backyard with friends, we can experience many opportunities for celebration during this season of fireworks, vacations, and longer days. Of course, summer can also be an incredibly busy time. If we're not careful, the summer months can speed by before we have a chance to look up.

No matter what might be going on in our lives, we could all use daily reminders of God's presence and providence. We can often get so caught up in thinking about the future that we completely miss what is happening in the present. You might be weighed down by the past, worried by the future, or even excited about something coming up, but all of these emotions can distract you from being fully present in the moment. And recognizing and celebrating the good immediately around us is impossible if we're not paying attention. But when we take the time to look for the good—to rejoice in the *today* that God has made—we will naturally begin to see him at work in our lives.

During this season, be sure to look outside your home and take time to enjoy the beauty of the natural world and the gift of community. We are surrounded by blessings worth celebrating, if we only would take the time to look for them.

Reimagine

What is one of your favorite memories of summer or one of your favorite parts of this season? Why do you think that is, and how can you recreate that experience in a meaningful way this summer?

Whether you prefer to be in your home or outside during the summer, what is one way you can cultivate a life-giving routine to enjoy the best parts of the season?

Outside In and Inside Out

Mixing It Up

Summer is my favorite time to really celebrate the beauty of the outdoors. I typically do this by following the simple principle of "outside in and inside out." Below you will find some examples of ways you can bring the outdoors inside your home, as well as ways you can bring what you do inside to the outdoors. This list is just a place to start, so don't be afraid to explore other unique ways of applying this principle.

Outside In

- Make sure there is some kind of plant in each room.
- Use a variety of natural textures and patterns in your decor, including stone, leather, straw, wood, and metal.
- Bring in wildflowers and plants that naturally grow during the season.
- Have fruits or vegetables on display.
- Find any opportunity to open your windows or curtains to let in natural light.
- Keep the house smelling fresh with lavender, rosemary, peppermint, lemongrass, essential oils, or candles.

Inside Out

- Prepare dinner outside by barbecuing or grilling.
- Have a picnic.
- Host a campfire with s'mores.
- Watch movies outside with popcorn and blankets.
- Play outdoor versions of games like Jenga, Connect 4, checkers, and bowling.
- Create an outdoor reading nook.

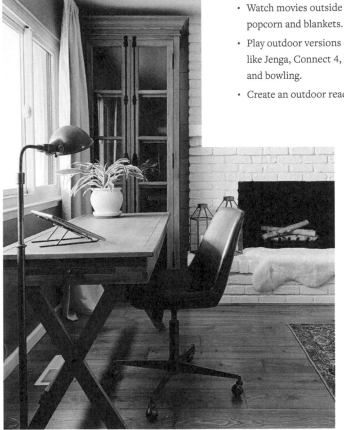

TASKS

Nature

You are the Lord, you alone. You have made heaven,
the heaven of heavens, with all their host, the earth and all
that is on it, the seas and all that is in them; and you preserve
all of them; and the host of heaven worships you.

—NEHEMIAH 9:6 (ESV)

AS MUCH AS I LOVE DECORATING the interior of my home, nothing quite compares to the joy of actually being outside in the world God created. I think this satisfaction stems in part from knowing that God carefully designed the natural world for us to enjoy. And compared to the other seasons of the year, summer is the one that most often invites us to spend time outside.

Even if you don't have access to a designated outdoor space, there are still many ways you can take advantage of the warmer weather while still experiencing the relaxation you would find at home. You can bring a book and a picnic blanket to a shaded park or set up a hammock between some trees. You can visit a community pool, help organize a neighborhood block party, or plan a night of stargazing in a friend's backyard. If you are fortunate enough to have your own outdoor area, you can be a blessing to others by hosting a backyard barbecue or even by creating an oasis retreat, complete with cushioned chairs, an umbrella, potted plants, and a cooler full of icy drinks.

Whatever your outdoor space looks like and however you decide to set it up, may it be a place where you can take in the wonderful sights and sounds of summer—in the company of others or on your own—while also serving as a reminder of God's gift to us.

Reimagine

*What is your favorite part
of nature or the outdoors that you
enjoy every summer?*

*How has nature connected
you to God?*

Outdoor Spaces
Shade, Seating, and Style

Whether you have your own backyard, an apartment courtyard, or a neighborhood park, make an effort this summer to spend some dedicated time outside. As you venture out into the sun or figure out how you would like to set up your outdoor space, try incorporating these three basic elements: shade, seating, and style.

Shade

Especially during the summer, curating some type of natural shade for your outdoor space is critical. So if you're camping or hanging out in a park, be sure to choose a spot beneath a tree or some other type of shade. If you're exploring a city, try wearing a floppy hat or sunglasses, or even open an umbrella. And when you're designing your own outdoor space, consider how you can take advantage of any trees you have or arrange some large, leafy potted plants where they can best provide shade. If natural shade isn't an option, you can create your own using an umbrella, canopy, or gazebo.

Seating

Once you have secured protection from the sun, figure out how you want to arrange seating, whether it's a hammock at the park, camp chairs on a road trip, or patio furniture on your back deck. If you like to host, comfy chairs and ample seating are essential features for creating a welcoming space for friends and family to relax with ice-cold drinks. Keep in mind that seating can range from a simple bistro table and chairs to benches, stumps, giant bean bags, hammocks, or a full patio dining set.

Style

With these basics set up, turn your attention to how you want to bring style into your outdoor area. If you're planning to spend time in a public outside space, maybe bring a colorful blanket, some music, or a stack of books. If you're curating your own backyard, one low-maintenance method of incorporating style is simply to enhance the natural elements that already exist. You can add signature plants or rocks or some kind of water or fire feature. These accents will help to clearly define the space as an area to enjoy the natural surroundings.

TRADITIONS
Habits

This is why I remind you to fan into flames the spiritual gift God gave you when I laid my hands on you.

—2 TIMOTHY 1:6 (NLT)

IN MOST AREAS of the United States, summer includes not only warmer days but also warmer nights. For our family, warm summer nights are definitely a favorite time to gather around a simple backyard campfire.

Now, anyone who knows how to properly make a campfire understands that how a fire is built can either make or break the experience for everyone. Using the wrong kind of wood, stacking it incorrectly, or not considering airflow can quickly turn the whole event into a smoky mess. When it comes to building a successful campfire, everything depends on proper preparation. Taking the time to get the right wood at the right sizes, and then carefully arranging them in the right way, makes it so much easier to keep a fire cleanly burning for a long time.

Building healthy habits into our lives is very similar to building a healthy fire. We can't just throw new habits into our lives at random and expect them to produce lasting results. We have to strategically stack right-sized habits with enough time and space to keep positive momentum. Ultimately, the healthy habits we create in our lives become a blessing to everyone around us— much like a fire casting an even glow around the circle. With enough planning and disciplined persistence, healthy habits can become positive lifestyles that influence and encourage those in our homes and communities.

Reimagine

What habits or lifestyles are
you hoping to kindle in your life?

What specific steps do you tend
to take when introducing a new rhythm
into your everyday routine?

Charcuterie Boards

Flavors of Summer

No campfire could be complete without roasting some marshmallows. In my family, we try to make this a very creative experience by making a s'mores charcuterie board. We start with the three basic ingredients: marshmallows, chocolate, and graham crackers. Then, we get creative with the rest of the options. Our favorites include peanut butter, chocolate graham crackers, cookies, and strawberries.

As you experiment with new flavors this summer, feel free to create your own s'mores board or come up with other charcuterie board ideas. This way of serving food can be an easy and cheap way to make a feast look instantly fancy.

S'mores Board

Ingredient Options

blueberries	Nutella
caramel sauce	Oreo cookies
fudge-striped cookies	raspberries
Ghirardelli chocolate caramel squares	Reese's peanut butter cups
Girl Scout cookies	stroopwafels
Hershey's cookies 'n' creme bar	

Other Board Ideas

Breakfast Board Pile your board with bacon, sausage, quiche, mini pancakes, fruit, toast, and other breakfast goodies.

Dessert Board Satisfy your sweet tooth with a board of to-die-for desserts, which could include mini cheesecakes, cookies, chocolates, mousse cups, brownies, or fruit tarts.

Taco Board Create a fun fiesta with build-your-own taco ingredients such as fajita meat, ground beef, diced tomatoes, avocado slices, shredded cheese, pico de gallo, guacamole, sour cream, lettuce, and salsa.

Snack Board Spruce up the after-school or after-work snack with a board of healthy or sweet-and-salty treats that could include carrot sticks, hummus, cucumber slices, pretzels, crackers, cheese, nuts, chips, popcorn, or chocolate.

Movie-Themed Board

Accompany your favorite movie with a snack board to match, whether that's Ring Pops, rosemary shortbread, and strawberries and cream for *Lord of the Rings* or braided pretzels, grapes, and hazelnut soup for *Tangled*.

Rustic Italian Board

Take a tour of Tuscany with a board decorated with crusty bread, olive oil, grapes, Italian cheese, olives, figs, tomatoes, and prosciutto.

Dinner Buffet Board

Simplify dinner with a buffet board that can include anything from build-your-own pizza to craft-your-own barbecue to mix-your-own mac 'n' cheese.

Date-Night Board

Go for fancy with wine and cheese or figure out yours and your date's favorite small bite options and create a board just for the two of you.

Cheese Board

All the cheese, all the time.

Omelet Board

Offer the omelet fixings on a beautiful display board and then whip up personalized omelets with ingredients like cheese, mushrooms, tomatoes, spinach, onions, and seasonings.

Country-Themed Board

Venture outside your comfort zone by choosing a country, researching its cuisine, and creating a board showcasing a cultural menu.

Monochromatic Board

Choose a single color like red, white, green, or yellow and arrange a board using only the foods that correspond to that particular color. See how creative you can get!

Rainbow Board Use the red-orange-yellow-green-blue-indigo-violet pattern to create a board featuring all the colors of the rainbow!

Holiday-Themed Board Bring a Christmas, Thanksgiving, or Easter-themed board to your next holiday gathering or potluck, using the tastes and decor of the season for inspiration.

Pizza Board Host a pizza night and pile all the toppings on fancy boards so that your guests have ready access to their preferred ingredients when building their own personal-size pizzas.

Bagel Board Craft a perfect brunch board with mini bagels or bagel halves, several flavors of cream cheese spread, sliced fruit, peanut butter, chocolate chips, avocado, and lox.

Hot Chocolate Board Cozy up on a cold day with a hot chocolate board, complete with marshmallows, chocolate stirring sticks, candy canes, chocolates, whipped cream, and flavored hot cocoa mixes.

TASTES

Togetherness

Let us think of ways to motivate one another to acts of love and good works. And let us not neglect our meeting together, as some people do, but encourage one another, especially now that the day of his return is drawing near.

—HEBREWS 10:24-25 (NLT)

POTLUCK. Depending on your experience, this word can bring either a smile to your face or a sense of anxiety to your spirit. Unfortunately, even though the intent of potlucks has always been the gathering of friends and family, they sometimes can turn into negative opportunities for stress and comparison. While we can't force others to experience potlucks the way they were meant to be, we can do something about our own perspective. After all, the most important thing that is shared in any potluck is not the food, but the company. If we can help gently remind others of that through our actions and attitudes, we can perhaps shift the focus away from who brought the best pie to how life-giving it is to be together.

Creating moments for and scheduling time to connect with family and friends is a simple yet important habit that can be incorporated into your home life. In the book of Hebrews, the author reminds us that we are all meant to live life together. In fact, God intentionally designed us both to give and to receive encouragement from one another. However, it is up to us to decide how we will gather and how we will respond to and treat those we find in our shared spaces.

This summer, whether with a potluck, game night, or watch party, do your best to schedule a time for cultivating community and transforming your own home into a space that can be shared.

Reimagine

Who in your life encourages you?
Who do you encourage?

How often does your home serve as
a place where people gather? What is one
event you can consistently host at your
home to bring people together?

Three-Bean Chili

A Summer Staple

If there is one entree that has become a potluck staple for our family, it is our three-bean chili. Whether on burgers, hot dogs, fries, nachos, or just in a bowl by itself, this chili is by far the most flexible dish that we make for all of our potlucks.

SERVES 6 TO 8

Prep time: 30 minutes

Cook time: 90 minutes

1 cup chicken broth

1 jar (25-ounce)
marinara sauce (plain)

1 can (15-ounce)
black beans, rinsed

1 can (15-ounce)
pinto beans, rinsed

1 can (15-ounce)
kidney beans, rinsed

1 tablespoon olive oil

1 medium white onion,
chopped

4 garlic cloves, minced

1 whole red bell pepper,
chopped

1 pound lean ground turkey

1½ teaspoons sea salt

½ teaspoon cumin

1 teaspoon oregano

1 package (1.25-ounce)
chili seasoning

In a slow cooker, add the broth, marinara sauce, and all the beans and stir to combine. Cover and turn on high heat.

In a large skillet heat the olive oil. Add the onion, garlic, and bell pepper and cook 3 to 5 minutes, until soft and fragrant. Add the ground turkey and cook until no longer pink. Be sure to stir and break the turkey into small chunks. Add the salt, cumin, oregano, and chili seasoning, and mix to combine.

Pour the skillet contents into the slow cooker, and mix. Cover tightly and cook on high for 2½ hours. When done, serve the chili with corn bread or use it as a topping for hot dogs or baked potatoes.

SIGHTS

Wonder

When I look at the night sky and see the work
of your fingers—the moon and the stars you set in place—
what are mere mortals that you should think about them,
human beings that you should care for them?

—PSALM 8:3-4 (NLT)

THOUGH SUMMER HOLDS MANY DELIGHTS, a particularly awe-inspiring one is the night sky. In most parts of the country, the warmer nights invite many to linger on the back porch, venture out for an evening drive with the windows rolled down, or even abandon the city altogether for the promise of camping under the stars. On these nights, when we can look up at the glittering constellations for hours without freezing, we are somehow better able to appreciate just how huge and grand the universe is and just how small we are in comparison. The psalmist adopts this very idea when trying to describe the humility and gratitude we should feel in light of God's great love for us.

Too often, we can forget to recognize the scope of our place in the universe as our perspective shrinks to the overwhelming demands and responsibilities of each day. That is why God is always calling us back to be in constant communication and relationship with him. And what a gift! To be known, loved, and immeasurably cared for by the same God who set the stars in the sky. Such knowledge should be not only humbling but also comforting as we face the hard, boring, or frustrating in our day-to-day. After all, no matter what we may have to handle in our own lives or fix in our homes, remembering that God has got the whole universe under control helps us to maintain a healthy perspective on what really matters. So even if you can't always keep up with the house chores, or your design aesthetic is not quite as Instagram-worthy as you'd like it to be, look up every once in a while and allow the stars to remind you that God's got this and that you are known and loved.

Reimagine

In what ways has worrying about
the appearance of your home "shrunk"
your perspective?

How are you making time and space
to appreciate the home God has
blessed you with?

How does your home serve as a
reminder of God's love and provision
for those who walk through your door?

A Healthy Home Perspective
Keeping It Real

With the overwhelming amount of interior design Instagram accounts, home renovation reality shows, and online listicles about how to create your magazine-worthy home, keeping a humble and healthy perspective of our own homes can be challenging. As much as we try to avoid thoughts of comparison, the little nagging messages that we are falling behind or not as put-together as everyone else can slip uninvited through the windows of our minds. The results, if we listen to these voices of envy, can lead to stress, anxiety, a lack of peace, financial insecurity, and other debilitating mindsets.

But the truth is that our homes should not look like everyone else's, nor like the photos we see filling our social media feeds. Our homes are unique reflections of who we are—sort of like a diary we allow others to read—and our individual likes, quirks, and passions should come across in everything from our collections to our decor. In the same way that creating a mask for yourself on social media leads to a false and unhealthy façade, constructing a "fake front" in your home can cause undue stress as you struggle to maintain an aesthetic that isn't true to who you are.

Of course, maintaining a healthy perspective and avoiding comparison is definitely easier said than done. But as you approach cultivating these healthy habits in your life, try responding to the following questions, either in a journal or with a trusted friend.

Recognizing the Good

- What is your favorite room or your favorite space in your home?
- What makes you enjoy this space?
- What does this space say about you?
- What keeps you from fully enjoying this space?
- How can you accentuate what you like about this space?

Dreaming about the Future

- What is your primary goal for your home right now? Is there a specific area or feature you would like to add, update, remove, renovate, or change?
- What is your inspiration behind this area of your home? Where did you get that inspiration?
- How do your goals for this area reflect your individual personality?
- How would you feel if your plans are delayed or if the final results don't match your vision? Dig into why you would feel that way.

Cultivating a Healthy Perspective

- When or where do you find yourself most susceptible to comparison when it comes to your home?
- What about your home makes you feel insecure?
- What about your home brings you joy and delight?
- How can you make a plan now for stopping comparison in its tracks the next time you're tempted to feel it?

Remembering Whose You Are

- How does your home reflect your unique identity?
- What serves as a reminder for you of your special place in God's creation?
- When do you most feel God's love for you?
- Make a list of the blessings in your home as it is now and of the provisions God has given you.

SOUNDS

Peace

*And he awoke and rebuked the wind
and said to the sea, "Peace! Be still!"
And the wind ceased, and there was a great calm.*

—MARK 4:39 (ESV)

WHAT WOULD SUMMER BE without the beach? Whether you have a coastline only minutes away or you have to drive or fly to reach one, the sandy shore, salty waves, and vibrant sunsets certainly feel like hallmarks of summer vacation.

Growing up around Monterey Bay, I always had easy access to a beautiful ocean view. I would spend summers exploring tide pools, building sandcastles, and running from waves. Because of these happy memories, I always feel calm at the beach. It's one of my favorite places to go when I need to reflect, get perspective, and find peace.

Even though the *sound* of waves can be soothing (to the point that many people even listen to it when falling asleep!), the reality of several thousand pounds of water crashing onto a shoreline is anything but gentle. The disciples discovered this when they were out on the Sea of Galilee and a giant storm sprang up. They woke Jesus in their terror, but he simply told the wind and sea: "Peace! Be still!" To the disciples' astonishment, the wind immediately died down and the sea became calm.

Our storms don't typically involve actual water, but we certainly face challenges like waves of uncertainty, torrents of hardship, and shifting tides of pain or loss. And even though we might not always sense it, Jesus still speaks "Peace! Be still!" over us today. The beauty of that promise is that Christ's peace is stronger than any feeling we might be facing, and is available even on our most stressful days. When we allow his peace to wash over our lives, we will find that the truest kind of calm enters our homes—no sound machine required.

Reimagine

In what area of your home
do you feel the most at peace?
How can you extend that feeling to
other rooms in the house?

Which specific "storms"
in your life do you need Jesus
to speak peace into?

Relaxation Spaces
A Peaceful Vibe

Regardless of its size, number of rooms, or roster of occupants, a home should always offer some measure of peace and represent a kind of personalized oasis from the world with its demands, responsibilities, and general rush. Home is where we can rest and recharge, where we can lower our guards and be fully ourselves. Home is where we should be able to take a breath before plunging into a new day. Where we live should act as a jumping-off point for stepping into the role and purpose God has called us to. After all, the safer and more comfortable we feel in our homes, the more equipped we will be to venture into the unknown of the outside world.

How has your home served as an oasis for you? How have you been able to cultivate a peaceful atmosphere both for yourself and for those who cross your threshold?

If your home doesn't feel like a refuge or retreat, or you simply need additional ideas to enhance the peacefulness of your home, use the list below to help:

- Play music to create a calm atmosphere.
- Prioritize and highlight your passions and the things that matter to you—both in your practical items and in your decor. In this way, your home can become not only unique to you but also a haven of all your favorite things.
- Store comfy blankets and pillows in a basket or cupboard or beneath a side table near your couches.
- Add candles for soft lighting to your bath routine, or try using an essential oil spray for your shower. You can even buy fresh eucalyptus to hang in your shower.

- Use candles or diffusers to introduce a relaxing environment. (Lavender, vanilla, sage, lemongrass, bergamot, ylang ylang, orange, chamomile, peppermint, and sandalwood are great scents for promoting relaxation!)

- Turn your bathroom into a luxurious spa where you can retreat at the end of a long day.

- Pull a comfy chair near to a bookshelf to create a cozy reading nook.
- Minimize clutter in common and living spaces.
- Keep the items you use the most in practical, easy-to-reach areas near to where you will use them.
- Organize tea bags in a basket or tea box and hang mugs on a mug tree to make an accessible drink station.
- At your desk, work area, or craft station, be sure to have your essentials handy and to also leave plenty of blank space for your projects or creativity. That way, when inspiration strikes, you don't have to spend time getting yourself organized.
- Decorate your shelves or walls with inspirational quotes, posters, family photos, fandom knickknacks, or travel memorabilia that hold special meaning for you.
- Find a place in your home where you can enjoy morning or evening quiet time while savoring a favorite drink.

SOCIALS

Freedom

Live as people who are free, not
using your freedom as a cover-up for evil,
but living as servants of God.

−1 PETER 2:16 (ESV)

IN ADDITION TO LONGER DAYS, warmer weather, and road-trip vacations, summer is marked by several important holidays in the American calendar, including Memorial Day, Juneteenth, and Independence Day. The last one has always been one of my favorites, particularly because of the opportunity it provides for my family to all come together, share sweet and savory food, and celebrate the gift of freedom we might take for granted on any other day of the year. Of course, I always enjoy watching the colorful fireworks displays, organizing the barbecues, participating in the fun outdoor games, and dressing in the old red, white, and blue. But all of these traditional activities are made sweeter and more memorable because they involve quality time with friends and family.

Due to an increasingly divisive culture and the impersonal type of interactions that are possible on social media, cultivating community is certainly becoming a challenge, while keeping others "at a distance" is becoming far too easy. This is why coming together truly offers one of the best ways to celebrate freedom on the Fourth of July. Rather than using this freedom as an excuse to do whatever we want to do, whenever we want to do it, we can approach this historic holiday as an opportunity to recognize the gift of community, serve others around us, and share through our words and actions what true freedom means. This, after all, is what God created us to do. As the apostle Peter reminds us, we are to live as people who are free, not by taking our freedom for granted or taking advantage of it, but by putting the needs of others before our own and helping to champion the cause of freedom for those who do not have it yet.

Since our homes are often a reflection of who we are, we can often be tempted to turn them into places that are self-serving. But just like the gift of freedom, we should view our homes as precious gifts that we can steward to serve others. So whenever you approach home design or renovation, try to keep in mind the unique ways your choices will welcome, encourage, and serve those who pass under your roof. Because freedom and community are gifts to be shared.

Reimagine

What are some freedoms that you can forget to be grateful for?

How can you use your home to serve others this week?

Cultivating Community

Opening Your Home

Though it can be tempting to think of our homes as "our own," we should try to remember that they are actually—like every other blessing we've received—gifts from God. And gifts are meant to be shared so that they can be a blessing to others. Of course, not all of us are natural hosts and many of us don't have the space or resources to organize events in our home very often, but we *can* all use our homes to cultivate community and provide encouragement for those around us. From fully kitted-out backyards and magazine-worthy kitchens to cozy couches and glasses of iced tea, each of us has something to offer if only we would take the time to notice it and invite someone else in to share it.

Tips for Stress-Free Hosting

- Have some kind of snack or simple meal prepared (dishes don't need to be big or fancy; even providing cookies or crackers and cheese helps guests feel seen, welcomed, and loved!).
- Provide juice, punch, tea, or coffee.
- Ensure you have plenty of seating— benches are great for exterior spaces, and stackable or easily portable chairs are helpful for the interior.
- Set up a long table or arrange several small folding tables either inside or outside.
- Create a good flow of space and "traffic" so guests don't feel locked in.
- Offer up your space but invite others to bring something to share, whether a board game or a food dish.
- Set out outdoor games such as Jenga Giant, kubb, cornhole, or ladder golf.

Ideas on How to Build Community

- Lead a weekly Bible study or a monthly book club.
- Plan a regular game or movie night.
- Organize an annual neighborhood block party or backyard barbecue for church or work friends.

- Host special event parties such as back-to-school outdoor movie nights, birthdays, cookie exchanges, tea parties, or holiday parties.

FALL

A Time to Gather

The believers met together in the
Temple every day. They ate together in their
homes, happy to share their food with joyful hearts.

—ACTS 2:46 (NCV)

FALL IS A SEASON of transitions. The leaves begin to change color, kids head back to school, and many of us begin the process of winterizing our homes. As we head into the period of extended rest that comes with winter, many of us also use this time to gather and share from the season's harvest. Somehow the nostalgic aromas drifting from the kitchen coupled with the scent of spiced candles and the extra heap of scarves and jackets on the coat rack serve as cozy reminders that life was never meant to be lived alone. Sure, fall can sometimes feel like the perfect season to minimize the social events and begin the hibernating process, but we should also set aside time to be in community with the people we love.

In Acts, we get a beautiful picture of how tightly knit the early church was. They frequently met in both large and small groups and even shared meals together with joyful and generous hearts. When someone was in need, everyone else banded together so that no one had to go without something.

This kind of life-giving community is exactly what we should strive for in our own lives. And our homes are the perfect place for us to start. Ultimately, our homes were never meant to be pretty showrooms that could only be admired from a distance. Instead, they are designed to be inviting places where people can feel welcomed, cared for, and loved.

During this fall season, don't be afraid to open your home as the place where people can gather and share life together. Great blessings can be found in positioning your home to serve the greater purpose of building relationships and community.

Reimagine

What makes you feel welcomed
or cared for when you visit
someone else's home?

How can you position your home
as a place where community can grow?

Arrangements and Amenities

Create a Welcoming Atmosphere

Opening up your home can be an intimidating thought for many people. Fortunately, if you focus on the two primary perspectives of arrangements and amenities, it will be much easier to create an inviting and thoughtful environment for your guests.

When it comes to arrangements, you want to observe the general rule of creating flow. From the time guests arrive, you want to make it easy for them to take their next steps. Upon entering your home, make sure that your guests have a clear pathway to the seating area or living room. Once in the seating area, make sure that there is some kind of focal point, such as a fireplace, television, or window. Additionally, be sure to arrange any sofas or chairs in a way that encourages conversation. Finally, make certain that your guests have clear pathways to both the kitchen and the bathroom. These small things make a huge difference and can make staying at your house a treat for others.

Amenities are the perfect complement to a well-designed arrangement. Here is a list of some helpful amenities, organized by area, that you can use to make your guests feel extra special:

Entryway

- floor mat to clean feet or take off shoes
- a clear place to hang jackets and place shoes
- pairs of clean socks for barefoot guests

Living Room

- coasters for drinks
- throw blankets
- not too many pillows
- subtle scent from candles or diffuser
- Wi-Fi password displayed in a small frame
- phone charger(s)
- a curated selection of books

Kitchen

- water or drink dispenser with cups
- snack tray or charcuterie board
- toothpick jar or bowl of mints
- napkins, paper towels, or tissues in easy reach

Bathrooms

(set these up in a small basket so guests know the items are there for their use)

- scented soap and lotion
- Poo-Pourri or deodorizer
- travel shampoo and conditioner
- washcloths, loofahs
- travel toothbrushes and toothpaste
- feminine products
- disposable razors

Bedrooms

(try making up your guest room as a mini-Airbnb!)

- snack basket, mints on the pillow, or bottles of water on the nightstand
- folded towels
- fun guest book for adding notes or Polaroids

TASKS

Intentionality

*Teach us to number our days, that
we may gain a heart of wisdom.*

—PSALM 90:12

AS FAR BACK AS I CAN REMEMBER, the fall season has always been one of the busiest seasons of the year for me. I think that much of it has to do with the start of the school year. In our house, so much of our yearly rhythms are influenced by the school schedule. In fact, being a parent of four school-age children, figuring out meal planning and lunch preparation and juggling schedules for sports and extracurricular activities is almost a job in itself. And even for those without children, our fast-paced culture has made life increasingly busy.

With all the unending tasks and overpacked schedules most of us face daily, developing healthy habits and routines are vital aspects of keeping our focus trained on the more important things in life. One of the ways my husband and I do this for ourselves and our family is by time-blocking in a shared calendar. For our household, this little trick has actually become a crucial tool for maintaining a simple, organized, and intentional home.

Your home is more than just your house. It is the entire environment and foundation from which you and your family do life together. As such, your home should be grounded with intentional living, which comes from scheduling your priorities and not just prioritizing your schedule. By time blocking in your calendar, you can not only get clear about your plans for the week, but more important, you can block off sacred time for the things that are the greatest blessing to your home.

Reimagine

What are the priorities you need
to schedule for your home?

What sacred things do you want
to make space for in your schedule?

Time Blocking
Prioritizing What Matters

While many people prioritize their schedule, few people schedule their priorities. This subtle shift has been a game changer for our family. Scheduling time for your priorities, on particular days of the week, can create a healthy rhythm that will ensure you always have time for what matters the most.

Take a look at the list of activities on the opposite page and decide what are the priorities for you. Suggested frequency for each is included in parentheses. Feel free to add or adjust as needed. Then evaluate your calendar and see where you can block off time for each item. Keep in mind it might save your weekends to spread chores throughout the week so you don't have to cram them all in on a Saturday. Additionally, if you live with family members or roommates, try to come up with a cleaning schedule so that no one gets stuck doing all the chores. Keeping a digital calendar or a whiteboard or corkboard in the kitchen is also helpful for visualizing the tasks for each week.

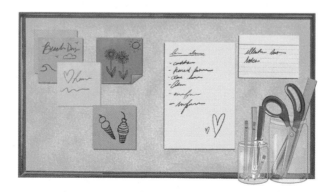

Spiritual Wellness

- morning or evening quiet time (daily)
- prayer (daily)
- lunch with a mentor or spiritual advisor (monthly or bimonthly)
- coffee with a friend, phone call to a family member, or some other soul-enriching one-on-one (weekly)
- Sabbath rest (weekly, whether on a Sunday or some other day!)
- Bible study, small group, potluck, or some other small communal activity (weekly or biweekly)
- church or other large spiritual gathering (weekly)

Mental Wellness

- reading, journaling, drawing, painting, or some other creative activity (3 to 4 times weekly)
- limiting screen time (weekly)
- outside time (daily)
- doing something you enjoy (weekly)

Physical Wellness

- walking, running, jogging, yoga, Pilates, swimming, gardening, lifting, gym activity, or some other form of physical exercise (daily)
- setting aside time for sleep (daily)
- meal prepping (daily or weekly)

Home Wellness

- kitchen dishes (daily or 3 to 4 times weekly)
- vacuuming or sweeping (weekly)
- dusting (biweekly)
- cleaning bathrooms (weekly)
- gardening, weeding, lawn mowing (weekly)
- reorganizing, minimizing, or decluttering (seasonally)
- laundry (daily or weekly)

TRADITIONS

God's Word

The grass withers and the flowers fade,
but the word of our God stands forever.

—ISAIAH 40:8 (NLT)

FALL IS MOST OFTEN signaled by the changing colors of the leaves, but in our family, one of our favorite traditions for marking the start of the season is by flower picking. We are so fortunate to have a nearby organic farm that grows a variety of flowers. On our first trip to the farm, we just chose any flower that looked nice at the moment, not realizing that certain flowers don't last very long after they have been cut. In fact, some of our flowers faded so fast, they didn't even survive the drive home.

Thankfully, our flower-picking process eventually took a turn for the better after we talked to one of the owners, who walked us through the process of how to dry flowers so they last longer. Since then, we have been able to keep some beautiful dried-flower arrangements in our home that are able to last throughout the whole fall season.

Of course, no matter how carefully a flower is dried, it will at some point lose its vibrance and crumble into pieces. As the prophet Isaiah explained, every flower eventually fades, but God's Word will last forever. Our homes might be sturdier than flowers, but they too are not built to last. And how often do we spend time or money on things that will ultimately fade away? How often do we instead prioritize God's plans and purposes?

Whenever you find yourself losing sight of what matters or what is most important, try turning to the Bible. Reading God's Word, and letting his Word read you, will always renew your perspective and should help give you the confidence you need to make a better decision.

Reimagine

What signals the start of fall for you?
Do you have favorite fall traditions?

What are the most common
things that get in the way of you
reading God's Word?

What is your favorite time to
consistently get into God's Word?

Flower Drying

DIY Decor

Florals bring life, vitality, and pops of color to your home decor, but buying fresh flowers can quickly become expensive. To keep your florals vibrant throughout the season and to limit how much you spend on them, try drying them. Simply bundle up your flowers into very small bouquets (so they do not mold). Then hang them upside down in a dark, dry room. After a couple weeks, you can spray them with hairspray and start making your arrangements.

Favorite Flowers to Dry

- amaranth
- baby's breath
- celosia
- gomphrena
- lavender
- lunaria
- pansy
- roses
- statice
- strawflower

How to Use Dried Flowers in Your Decor

- Arrange them in vases on tables, credenzas, mantels, or shelves.
- Tie them to wire, ribbon, or string and hang them to create a flower wall.
- Gather the buds or petals in bowls to place in bathrooms, on coffee tables, or near the front door.
- Store your dried flowers in dark (not clear) bins or boxes (they should keep fairly well!).

In case you're not into DIY, or feel you don't have time, consider shopping for dried flowers at your local florist. Many florists and nurseries sell dried flowers and plants—sometimes already bundled in lovely arrangements!

TASTES

Imitation

Remember your leaders, who spoke
the word of God to you. Consider the outcome
of their way of life and imitate their faith.

—HEBREWS 13:7

THESE DAYS, pumpkin has become practically synonymous with fall. Our family loves going to the pumpkin patch and choosing pumpkins to help decorate the house. But beyond setting up pumpkins as table centerpieces or porch ornaments, our family also loves using them to bake our favorite fall dessert—pumpkin muffins.

My passion for pumpkin-flavored baked goods started when I had my first pumpkin loaf while working at Starbucks. Something about that moist cake, with its ideal balance of cinnamon and pumpkin, left me desperately wanting to replicate it for myself. After many failed attempts, I finally found the perfect recipe, which I now use for both pumpkin loaves and muffins. (Of course, with a family of six in the home, I tend to make more muffins now since they seem to last longer than loaves do when there are a lot of people!) These easy-to-make and easy-to-share treats have definitely become part of our family's fall tradition, but I never would have made them if it had not been for that job at Starbucks.

Unfortunately, despite my positive result with the pumpkin muffins, imitation can often come with a negative stigma. Most of us don't like the idea of copying something, buying imitation products, or adopting unoriginal practices in our homes. However, when viewed another way, imitation is the sincerest form of flattery. After all, we shouldn't be embarrassed to borrow home decor ideas from friends or style experts, and we shouldn't be offended if others adopt ideas from our homes. Whenever someone copies one of my home tips, I feel honored!

For believers, imitation is one of our highest callings. All throughout Scripture, we are encouraged to imitate Christ and those that follow him. This isn't the same as having an "idol" you look up to. Rather, we should look for those who are actively walking with God and view their best actions as examples we can imitate. Though it may sound a little strange, God has designed us from birth to find leaders around us to follow. So don't be embarrassed to follow the good leaders around you, and don't be afraid to lead others in specific arenas that are important to you—whether that is in baking tips, home design ideas, or a life of faith.

Reimagine

What was your last enjoyable
experience with an "imitation"?

Who are the people in your life
that are worth imitating?

In what areas of your life do you
see others imitating you? How
does that inspire you?

Pumpkin Muffins
Almost Like Starbucks

MAKES

2 dozen muffins

Prep time: 20 minutes

Cook time: 20 minutes

2 cups pure pumpkin puree (canned or fresh)

3 cups granulated sugar

1 cup canola or vegetable oil

4 large eggs

3⅓ cups all-purpose flour

2 teaspoons baking soda

1½ teaspoons salt

1 teaspoon ground cinnamon

1 teaspoon ground nutmeg

Preheat the oven to 350°F for a nonstick muffin pan. Line the muffin pan with paper muffin cups or spray with nonstick spray.

In a large mixing bowl, mix the pumpkin, sugar, oil, ⅔ cup water, and eggs until well combined.

In a medium mixing bowl, combine the flour, baking soda, salt, cinnamon, and nutmeg. Whisk until well combined.

Gradually pour the flour mixture into the pumpkin mixture. Stir well to combine completely.

Pour the batter evenly into the muffin cups.

Bake for 18 to 20 minutes, or until a toothpick inserted into the center of a muffin comes out clean (baking time will vary based upon your oven, the type of pan, and your elevation).

Once done, transfer the muffins to wire racks and allow to cool.

Once the muffins have completely cooled, ENJOY!

SIGHTS

Trust

But blessed are those who trust in the Lord and have made the Lord their hope and confidence. They are like trees planted along a riverbank, with roots that reach deep into the water. Such trees are not bothered by the heat or worried by long months of drought. Their leaves stay green, and they never stop producing fruit.

—JEREMIAH 17:7-8 (NLT)

WHEN LEAVES BEGIN turning color and falling into delicate piles across the ground, you know without a doubt that fall has arrived. This beautiful phenomenon is especially visible in areas of the country that have deciduous trees, which transition into fiery canvases of vibrant oranges, reds, and yellows. And then, almost overnight, the leaves have all fallen and gone dry, leaving the trees bare for the winter.

It can be shocking how quickly the seasons come and go. Change happens when we least expect it and before we feel we are ready for it. But that's part of life, isn't it? Just as God designed creation to experience seasons, he designed us to be able to withstand lives of constant shifts and changes. One of the most important ways he equipped us to endure life's transitions was in giving us himself—a God who is unchanging. As the prophet Jeremiah describes it, those who place their trust, hope, and confidence in the Lord are like trees that are planted by a river. Unlike deciduous trees, their leaves do not fall or dry up because they have a constant resource strengthening and sustaining them, even during the most destructive floods or stormy winds.

For those who place their trust in the Lord, life can be exactly like that tree Jeremiah described. The world around us will still constantly change, and we will still have to adjust as different hurdles and challenges are thrown our way, but our character and confidence can remain constant as we root our trust in a saving relationship with God.

As you journey through this fall season, think about who you are placing your trust in or what you are setting your hopes on. Does your home serve as an accurate reflection of those hopes?

Reimagine

*What parts of your home
change in the fall?*

*Where in your life are you going
through a season of change?*

*How can you place your trust in
God during this season?*

Seasonal Checklists
Navigating Change

Spring

- Service the sprinkler system.
- Fertilize the lawn.
- Plant flowers.
- Have the roof checked.
- Service the air conditioner, furnace, or home-filtration system.
- Spring-clean the closets, garage, or other clutter-prone areas.
- Repaint and reseal weather-damaged surfaces.
- Reinstall window screens if removed for the winter.
- Consider home upgrades and make a plan and budget for any summer projects.

Summer

- Stage outdoor furniture.
- Prep the grill or campfire and stock up on wood or coal.
- Have the home's interior and exterior serviced against insects.
- Perform safety checks.
- Reverse ceiling fan rotations to allow for downward cooling.
- Deep clean appliances such as washing machines, dishwashers, and disposals.
- Power-wash decks, driveways, patios, or other hard surfaces.
- Wipe down baseboards and ceiling fans.
- Invest in a summer home project.

Fall

- Switch out summer wardrobe for winter clothes.
- Sweep off roof or get the roof checked professionally.
- Service fireplace, flue, and chimney.
- Blow out sprinkler system and turn off.
- Replace the furnace filter and have the furnace serviced.
- Change the batteries on smoke and carbon monoxide detectors.
- Bring in outdoor plants (before temperatures drop below 45°F).

Winter

- Clear out gutters.
- Store outside furniture, cushions, or blankets.
- Cover the grill.
- Close outdoor vents.
- Cover plants.
- Turn off all pipes and disconnect hoses.
- Check for drafts or gaps in windows or under doors.
- Remove window screens.
- Caulk any leaks and check the insulation.
- Stock up on batteries, flashlights, and a snow shovel or ice scraper.
- Keep blankets in your car.

SOUNDS

Redemption

Sing, O heavens, for the LORD has done it;
shout, O depths of the earth; break forth into singing,
O mountains, O forest, and every tree in it! For the LORD
has redeemed Jacob, and will be glorified in Israel.

—ISAIAH 44:23 (ESV)

THE FALL SEASON is by far my favorite time to go hiking. I love how the weather is not too hot or too cold, and how there is just enough of a cool breeze to make nature seem even more alive. We are fortunate to have several hiking trails nearby, but my favorite kind of location is in the mountains or a forest. Walking through the beautiful trees is such a peaceful experience, and looking out over lush valleys stirs up so much awe and wonder for me.

It truly is amazing how something as silent as nature can say so much. But the more time I spend in nature, the more I tend to hear God's voice. I love the passage in Isaiah where he describes every part of creation as singing and shouting praise to God for the gift of redemption. How wonderful to think that as beautiful as our world is, a new creation is coming that will be even better!

Both managing a house and keeping its design aesthetic fresh can feel like unending challenges, but they do not have to be all-consuming. As we go about each day, we should remember that our lives and responsibilities here on earth are only temporary. Of course, we should always be thankful for the ways God has blessed us and give our best effort to the unique callings he has given us, but ultimately he is responsible for taking all of the broken and flawed parts of our world and transforming them into something perfect. With that in mind, we should always live open-handed with everything we have in this life, even our homes.

Reimagine

What parts of your home have been
"redeemed" or restored? Or
which parts need to be?

In what areas of your life are
you still awaiting redemption
from Christ?

Restoring and Repurposing

Making the Old New

Even if you're not into DIY, you can still restore or repurpose different features in your home without spending too much money or pulling your hair out. And the principle of "making the old new" is a great way to add a bit of freshness and visual interest to your home without blowing your budget. If you need specific ideas for inspiration, check out the list of tips below:

- Chalk paint offers a wonderfully simple way to repaint furniture. It doesn't require a lot of preparation work, and it has a highly durable finish.

- Changing up your pillow shams or throw blankets can quickly provide a new look to a room. If you're handy with a sewing machine, you can even save money by making your own shams!

- Greenery and florals are, unsurprisingly, lovely ways to spruce up and refresh a room. Certain plants also come with amazing health benefits, such as offering a free air purifier for the room.

- If you have a lot of artwork on your walls, try switching out the frames. You can find cheap frames at thrift stores or antique shops. These can either be repainted or displayed in all of their vintage glory!

- Decorative mirrors are another great item to pick up at an antique store, since they add a nice touch to any room. Water-based stains work great on the frames, and you can buff the mirror surfaces until they shine.

- If you have a TV in your living area or family room, you can try framing it to turn it into a somewhat decorative piece. You can also find free digital screensavers to display on the screen when it's not in use.

- Painting an accent wall can completely change the atmosphere of a room. Though it does require a little more effort on your part, it can be a relatively inexpensive way to make a room look renovated.

- Blank walls always have great decorative potential. In our home, we have a wall that changes themes depending on the season. We use a projector to trace out the word for that season, and then I paint it in. You could personalize your own blank wall with theme words, floating bookshelves, a photo collage, or a flower wall.

- If you live in an apartment or don't want to paint on a wall, buy a large blank canvas and add a splash of color that you can switch out as needed!

SOCIALS
Gratitude

*I will give thanks to the L*ORD* with my whole heart;*
I will recount all of your wonderful deeds.

—PSALM 9:1 (ESV)

AH, THANKSGIVING. A holiday that usually means good food, good community, and maybe a Black Friday shopping spree. During this season, airports experience one of their busiest times of the year, over forty-five million turkeys are purchased, and more than five billion dollars are spent on online shopping. Between the extended time with friends and family and the bountiful leftovers stocked in the fridge, this holiday clearly has a lot of perks to offer.

Sadly, Thanksgiving can also be a very difficult time of year. For many, the season brings with it a reminder of past loss. For others, family tensions that have long been simmering might flare up over the dinner table. And even for those who look forward to the Thanksgiving feast, preparations, planning, and costs can certainly contribute to no small amount of stress. Most, if not all, of these factors lie outside our control, and we can't simply split a turkey wishbone and make all the sad or hard parts disappear. So what can we do? How should we approach such a major holiday to have a positive experience?

At the risk of sounding obvious, let's look again at the original purpose of Thanksgiving. And no, I don't mean the meal that was shared between the Indigenous Americans and Pilgrims back in 1621. I'm talking about the biblical calling of giving thanks, which is mentioned over one hundred times in Scripture. Clearly, offering praise and thanksgiving is important. But why? Well, for one, God created us to praise him, and when we participate in thanksgiving, we fulfill part of our purpose here on earth. Giving praise also draws us nearer to God and, by default, to the larger community of believers. As if those weren't reasons enough, cultivating a posture of gratitude is also good for our health (Proverbs 17:22).

In our current culture, so much energy is spent on criticizing and complaining, rather than on being thankful. Part of the issue stems from the fact that when we place ourselves and our own desires above God, the good in our lives can become hazy or muddled. But when we make the intentional choice to "give thanks in all circumstances"—especially when things are hard or challenging—God grants us the gift of a renewed perspective. Our situations may not improve overnight, but our attitudes will. And who knows? Maybe our act of choosing joy will help brighten the lives of those around us.

Whatever your experience has been with Thanksgiving in the past, I pray that you will be able to find occasion for gratitude and that the resulting renewal of your mind will make this year a special celebration for yourself and for those you gather around you.

Reimagine

What has Thanksgiving been like in your home? How would you like it to be?

When do you find it hard to be grateful?

How can you encourage others into a spirit of gratitude this season?

Thanksgiving Tree
An Attitude of Gratitude

One way we try to highlight our gratitude at Thanksgiving is by making our celebration last for the entire month. We do this by putting up a Thanksgiving tree at the beginning of November. Every day we decorate it with simple ornaments on which we write one thing we are thankful for. We even invite our friends and other house guests to add their own notes of thankfulness. By the end of the month, we have created a tree full of gratitude and, more important, have renewed an excellent habit. Try creating your own Thanksgiving tree or other tradition of counting your blessings so that you can realign your perspective and be reminded of how truly good God is. You can use a real tree, buy a small fake one, craft a little wooden one, or even make one out of paper.

Kickstart Ideas

- Create an alarm on your phone that reminds you to write something every day.

- Place random tags around the house and write something every time you find one.

- Bring tags with you to work, or while running errands, and ask someone else to write something for your tree.

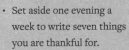

- Set aside one evening a week to write seven things you are thankful for.

- At the end of the season, place the tags or ornaments in a jar that you can return to whenever you need a reminder of your blessings until you start the tradition again the next Thanksgiving.

If you love your little Thanksgiving tree, feel free to redecorate it and reuse it for holidays throughout the year!

WINTER

A Time to Rest

Then Jesus said, "Come to me, all of you who are weary
and carry heavy burdens, and I will give you rest."

—MATTHEW 11:28 (NLT)

IN NATURE, WINTER has always served as a time of rest. Most living things go into a period of hibernation, when they focus on conserving their energy for the coming spring season. Unfortunately, this natural process of resting is not mirrored in our human society. As winter begins, we often become preoccupied with ever-growing to-do lists, shopping lists, "new year, new you" lists, and more. In the end, we can turn out looking more like human *doings* than human *beings*. To make matters worse, we become increasingly bombarded with all of the marketing and merchandising associated with Christmas so that the winter season ends up being one of the most stressful times of the year.

Jesus understood firsthand the weariness and heaviness that busyness can bring to our lives. But rather than telling us off for trying to do or be too much, he instead offers himself as the source of ultimate rest for our souls. When we surrender our tight-fisted control and accept his gift of peace and an "easy yoke," we will be able to experience true rest—even when situations around us are still crazy.

If you think about it, the fact that the one season when we should experience the most rest from the presence of Jesus is also the time when we are tempted to be at our busiest is no coincidence. The Enemy, after all, knows how to catch us when we're down. Because of that, we should be even more vigilant during this "most wonderful time of the year." So, this winter season, try to protect your home from becoming a place of anxiety and stress. Instead, give it over to God and ask him to make it a peaceful oasis of welcome and renewal, where people can experience the rest that only Jesus can provide.

Reimagine

What parts of your home give
you the greatest sense of peace?

How can your home offer a haven
of peace to others?

Where can you say "no"
this season to give yourself greater
margin for peace?

Warm and Cozy
Delighting the Senses

When designing our homes to produce a particular kind of feeling, one of the best places to start is with the senses. During the winter season, our sense of touch and taste get impacted the most. This is why I use the simple rule of "warm and cozy" as a way to bring a much-needed peace and rest to this frigid season. Below you will find some easy ways that you can begin incorporating both warm and cozy things into your home design.

Warm Things

- making baked goods
- cooking soups and stews
- brewing coffee or hot chocolate
- treating yourself to long, luxuriant bubble baths
- lighting the fireplace
- burning candles
- keeping a fluffy blanket draped over the back of the couch for easy access

Cozy Things

- adding fleece or fur throws
- using flannel pillowcases and bedsheets
- putting a fluffy, down duvet on top of bedding
- wearing fleece-lined slippers
- creating a reading nook
- building a pillow fort
- having plenty of fleece socks available

TASKS

Humility

Though he was God, he did not think of equality
with God as something to cling to. Instead,
he gave up his divine privileges; he took the humble
position of a slave and was born as a human being.
When he appeared in human form, he humbled
himself in obedience to God and died a
criminal's death on a cross.

—PHILIPPIANS 2:6-8 (NLT)

FOR OUR FAMILY, one of the first tasks of the winter season is breaking out our Advent calendar. The tradition of counting down the days until Christmas with little chocolates or other treats has become somewhat commercial and mainstream these days, but the heart of it goes back to the New Testament, when Jesus told his followers to wait and keep watch for his return. In this way, believers celebrate Advent for two reasons: as a remembrance of Jesus's first coming as a baby and as a reminder to keep ourselves ready for his second. In light of the former, not a year goes by that I am not completely humbled and overwhelmed with gratitude when I think about the Creator of the universe leaving his place in heaven to come down to earth, walk alongside us, and ultimately give his life for all of humanity. Of course, I try to keep this in mind throughout the year, but somehow the weight of it feels more tangible during the Christmas season.

Because of its focus on humility, one of my favorite passages to read during Advent is the poem Paul includes in his letter to the Philippians. The passage reminds us that Jesus himself did not shy away from giving up his divine privileges and instead took on the humble form of a servant because of his great love for us. If the Son of God lowered himself to such a vulnerable position for the sake of the world, we should follow his example by adopting a posture of humility and serving others—throughout the year, of course, but certainly at Christmas.

To be sure, Christmas is such a busy time, and we can easily forget to notice others as we allow ourselves to get wrapped up in our own schedules, party plans, and gift shopping. Sometimes we can become so consumed with ourselves that we get frustrated when we encounter "interruptions" or people that need our help. But Jesus himself was constantly running into interruptions in his ministry, and he always took the time to pause and notice those around him. In this very busy season, let us not forget his example and the truth that humility always ends in serving others. After all, the greatest Servant humbled himself for our benefit, so what else can we do than humble ourselves by serving those around us?

Reimagine

How can you cultivate a greater
posture of humility when it comes to
serving others with your home?

How does the humility of Jesus
inspire you to serve others?

Who can you humbly serve this week?

Advent Calendar

Christmas Daily

An Advent calendar brings such an exciting twist to the winter season. Whether with little chocolates, mini-ornaments, or other treats, using these calendars to count down the days until Christmas can help increase the sense of anticipation and coming celebration. Though many Advent calendars have become commercialized, the original intent of teaching us to practice a posture of joyful waiting is still there. As we look forward to Christmas, we are able to experience a taste of what it means to look forward to Jesus's eventual return.

Whether you observe Advent or not, check out the list of Advent activities below and try to incorporate them into your celebrations this season. Feel free to pick and choose, mix up the order, and even add your own ideas.

Advent Activity Ideas

- Text a friend to tell them why you are grateful for them.
- Draw, paint, or color something Christmas related.
- Write down your goals for the coming year.
- Buy coffee or lunch for someone.
- Show a random act of kindness.
- Make a random treat for your neighbors.
- Build a unique Christmas craft.
- Bake a special holiday treat to share with someone.
- Give a handwritten card or note to someone.
- Design a custom ornament for your tree.
- Dance to Christmas music.
- Eat dinner by candlelight.

- Give your favorite Christmas song new lyrics.
- Go sledding or ice-blocking.
- Plan a holiday gift exchange.
- Bring gifts or baked goods to a senior living community.
- Go caroling.
- Decorate cookies or gingerbread houses.

- Volunteer with Angel Tree, Operation Christmas Child, or another ministry.
- Invite someone over for dinner.
- Read through the Christmas story.
- Learn about a Christmas tradition from another country.
- Create a hot chocolate bar.
- Watch a Christmas movie with your family or friends.

TRADITIONS

Generosity

Whoever is generous to the poor lends to the Lord,
and he will repay him for his deed.

—PROVERBS 19:17 (ESV)

REGARDLESS OF ONE'S FAITH background, Christmas is almost universally recognized as a season of giving and goodwill to others. As a result, one of the most popular Christmas traditions around the world is that of giving gifts to others. Unfortunately, the practice of gift giving can quickly turn from a *good* thing to a *god* thing, which happens whenever we idolize giving the best or perfect gift. I have both observed and experienced the cultural pressure to give and receive increasingly extravagant gifts each year. The result of this kind of competitive generosity is that instead of giving out of love, we end up giving out of pride.

One way we have encouraged our family to have a better perspective on generosity during the Christmas season is to give gifts to those from whom we have no expectation of receiving a gift in return. Sometimes this means donating financially to certain organizations, or preparing gifts for specific people. Somehow, "seeing" or even knowing the person who will receive the gift makes the giving that much more meaningful and personal. Because of that deeper connection, our family enjoys participating in programs like Operation Christmas Child through Samaritan's Purse. We also take delight in helping those who might not be able to afford their own Christmas tree or dinner.

However you decide to practice generosity this season, try to prioritize giving not from a place of competition or compulsion but rather from a place of charity. After all, everything we will ever give to anyone else has already first been given to us by God. So during this season of giving, make sure your home remains a launching point of generosity for a world in need of God's love.

Reimagine

What kind of gifts are your favorite
to give or receive?

What in your home could be used or
given in service of others?

How can you cultivate a greater
spirit of generosity this Christmas?

Table Settings and Hosting Tips
Blessing Others at Christmas

With all the shopping to be done and the many parties to attend, the holidays can be a stressful time. Anxiety levels can rise even further when you're the one who has to host. Suddenly, you're responsible for the menu, the decorations, the guest list, the order of events, and the background music! Thankfully, much of the hosting burden can become lighter and even more fun when you apply this easy acronym: **H**ospitality, **O**penness, **S**implicity, and **T**heme.

Hospitality: *make guests feel welcome*

- Napkins can always add a bit of special flair and make your guests feel extra-special without much work on your part. If you have cloth napkins, try looking up a video tutorial on how to fold them. If using paper napkins, put them in a stack and then push down and twist on the top of the pile with a fist or the base of a glass.

- Adding name cards, though not necessary, can be a fun way to make guests feel welcome and seen, especially if you are going for a more formal atmosphere.

- If you're serving a potluck or buffet-style meal, informational cards by each serving dish can help clear any confusion about what each food item is. This is especially helpful if any of your guests have food allergies or intolerances.

- Be sure guests know what to expect when they arrive at your house. Is your house easy to find? Does it offer accessible parking?

- When guests arrive, make it clear where they should leave coats, bags, or shoes.

Openness: *be honest about what you can handle*

- If you're feeling overwhelmed, be honest with yourself and with others about your limits. Focus on readying your home and maybe providing the drinks or the games, but invite your guests to bring different dishes to share. If you don't know all the guests well, ask those you do know to help supply meal options.

- Remember the adage that two is better than one, and that a cord of three strands is not quickly broken. So don't be shy about inviting a friend or two to share the responsibility of cohosting with you!

Simplicity: *practice quality over quantity*

- Instead of using a full tablecloth, try decorating the table or other surfaces with a simple runner. Remember that bare wood can look nice, too!

- If you don't have enough matching plates or glasses, go for a purposeful "mismatched" theme. Or keep it really simple and use decorative disposable plates and utensils.

- When it comes to table decor, simple is almost always better, since it leaves more space for serving dishes and plates. You can decorate with a pair of candles, or arrange flowers, gourds, or greenery depending on the season.

- Decorative placemats or serving dishes can add a festive accent to your table if you decide to skip having a centerpiece.

- Unless you are an accomplished chef, steer away from trying out new recipes when you're hosting. If there is a special dish you'd like to serve, test it out before the night of the event so you can iron out any kinks or surprises with the recipe.

- Keep the menu simple! It's better to nail it on a few choice dishes than to try to create an elaborate feast with several average items.

Theme: *determine the goal of the event*

- Knowing the intent of the party or gathering is crucial for the host to pinpoint *before* the guests start to arrive. Is it a simple meet-and-greet or a casual mix-and-mingle? Is it an opportunity for deeper connection or a way to say "thank you" or "I'm here for you"? Whatever your theme, recognizing it early and making it your focus can help you maintain a proper perspective even if things don't all go according to plan. After all, if your guests feel seen, loved, or welcomed, it won't matter much if you run out of drinks, if an appetizer gets burned, or if an unexpected rain shower keeps you all inside.

- Once you know your "internal" theme, make sure you tell your guests what the "external" theme is so they know what to expect. Is it a game night? Are you serving a whole dinner or just hors d'oeuvres? Should guests bring anything or wear anything specific? Giving guests a heads-up can help put them more at ease before they even grace your door.

TASTES
Sharing

Do not neglect to do good and to share what you have,
for such sacrifices are pleasing to God.

—HEBREWS 13:16 (ESV)

HAVING GROWN UP IN a Mexican tradition, I experienced a wide variety of dishes associated with the winter season, including *tamales, pozole, ponche,* and *champurrado.* But my favorite by far has always been *puerquitos,* or Mexican pig-shaped gingerbread cookies. These soft and subtly sweet cookies have just the right touch of cinnamon and ginger and are always perfect when paired with a cup of coffee, a glass of milk, or a mug of hot chocolate.

Because I am constantly adding to my family's list of home traditions, I am always on the hunt for recipes of my favorite dishes. Unfortunately, it really took me a long time to find a recipe that was just right for these little puerquitos. I had almost given up hope when a friend of mine sent me a batch of gingerbread cookies that were exactly what I had been searching for. They were so delicious that I initially hesitated to ask her for the recipe. But when I did, my generous friend had no reservations about sharing, and I was finally able to add my favorite dessert to our home menu.

Sharing an original or family recipe may not seem like much of a sacrifice, but my friend's sweet action serves as a beautiful example of the biblical call to do good for others and share what we have. Even the smallest gifts can be a "pleasing aroma" to God, whether that's a plate of cookies for a neighbor, an unexpected present for a coworker, or an invitation given to friends or family to come and stay for the holidays. As a parent, I love seeing my children sharing what I have provided for them to enjoy, and I am certain that our heavenly Father feels the same way when we share with each other—even if it is a simple recipe.

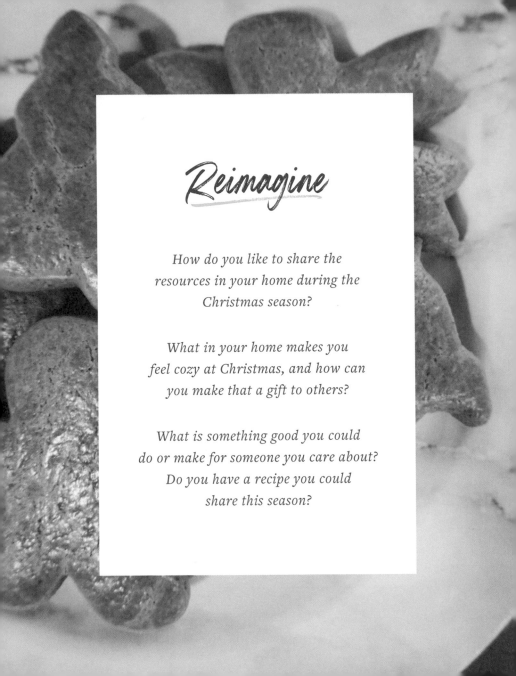

Reimagine

How do you like to share the
resources in your home during the
Christmas season?

What in your home makes you
feel cozy at Christmas, and how can
you make that a gift to others?

What is something good you could
do or make for someone you care about?
Do you have a recipe you could
share this season?

Puerquitos
Mexican Gingerbread

MAKES

2 dozen cookies

Prep time: 20 minutes

Cook and cool time:
20 minutes

½ cup unsalted butter,
softened

1 cup dark brown sugar,
packed

2 large eggs

¾ cup unsulfured molasses

¼ cup milk

½ teaspoon vanilla extract

5 cups all-purpose flour,
plus more for the work
surface

½ teaspoon baking soda

½ teaspoon ground
cinnamon

½ teaspoon ground ginger

Preheat the oven to 350°F. Line a cookie sheet with parchment paper and set aside.

In the bowl of a stand mixer (regular bowl with electric mixer works too), cream the butter until smooth, then add the brown sugar and beat until smooth. Add 1 of the eggs, the molasses, milk, and vanilla, and mix until combined.

In a separate large bowl, add the flour, baking soda, cinnamon, and ginger. Mix together to combine. Add the dry ingredients into the wet ingredients, a cup at a time, and mix until well combined. The dough should cleanly pull away from the mixing bowl.

Transfer the dough onto a lightly floured surface and roll out to slightly less than ½-inch thick. Use a pig-shaped cookie cutter (sometimes I like to change the shape to make it more interesting for the kids) to cut the dough into pigs.

In a small bowl, crack open the remaining egg and whisk. Brush the beaten egg over the tops of the pigs using a pastry brush.

Bake for 10 to 12 minutes, until the edges are lightly browned. Remove from the oven and transfer the cookies onto cooling racks. Cool for 10 to 15 minutes and enjoy!

SIGHTS
Light

You are the light of the world—like a city on
a hilltop that cannot be hidden. No one lights a
lamp and then puts it under a basket. Instead,
a lamp is placed on a stand, where it gives light
to everyone in the house. In the same way,
let your good deeds shine out for all to see, so that
everyone will praise your heavenly Father.

—MATTHEW 5:14-16 (NLT)

WITH THE ARRIVAL OF WINTER comes colder weather and darker nights. Though the shorter days can feel like a loss, the longer periods of darkness provide the perfect backdrop for my favorite element of home decor for this season: light. Light comes in many forms, including candlelight, twinkle lights, tree lights, star light, and firelight. Each of these forms of light offers a unique point of beauty in themselves, and they also illuminate everything around them. In fact, the darker the surroundings, the more brilliantly the light shines.

Light's special way of piercing through the darkness stands as a perfect metaphor for how we as believers should influence the world. After all, when Jesus was born in a stable in Bethlehem, the star in the sky wasn't the only new source of light on earth. Jesus himself brought a light to quench all darkness, and when we walk in the light, we are keeping in step with him and continuing his mission of love to the world. With Christ in us, we are lights, and we shouldn't let peer pressure, fear, intimidation, or the desire to fit in keep us from sharing that light with our communities. Just as light affects everything it touches, our connection with God should create an impact wherever we go, whatever we say, whatever we do, and whoever we spend time with.

As you come up with ways to add light to your home decor this Christmas, be sure to consider which areas of your life or your home might not be aligned with the light of Christ. Pray over those areas and ask for God's truth and grace to shine through you and your home, so that you can better serve the people around you.

Reimagine

What is your favorite kind of light?

Where can you add light to
your home decor?

Where do you need the light of
Christ to shine in your heart?

Winter Glow

Decorating with Light

Aside from having traditional Christmas lights outside our house, I really enjoy incorporating small candles and twinkle lights inside our home as well. Whether adding a splash of light to some eucalyptus garland, highlighting a ceramic village, or illuminating a birchwood fireplace, twinkle lights have become one of my favorite ways to add light all throughout the home.

Here are some specific ways to add light into your home:

- Use at least three different types of lighting in each room to add to the aesthetic (overhead lights, table lamps, floor lamps, candles, fairy lights, artistic bulbs, etc.)
- Place different-sized candles or lanterns in the fireplace, arranged either alone or in between birch wood logs
- Hang fairy lights in the seam between the wall and ceiling
- Set lamps on bathroom or kitchen counters
- Keep patio lights draped along a fence, beneath the eaves, or over a gazebo or porch
- Install solar lights in the garden or along the footpath

SOUNDS

Hope

And the angel said to them, "Fear not, for behold,
I bring you good news of great joy that will be for
all the people. For unto you is born this day in the city
of David a Savior, who is Christ the Lord."

—LUKE 2:10-11 (ESV)

WHAT WOULD WINTER BE without Christmas music? From jolly favorites on the radio to vinyl classics at home to jazzy new songs over the mall loudspeakers, Christmas music certainly provides a near-constant soundtrack to the holiday season. And while every family has its own "rules" on when it's appropriate to start listening to these songs, we can all most likely agree that the Christmas genre of music carries with it a happiness, nostalgia, and hope that is rare to find in other musical styles.

Hope defines not only Christmas music but the entire season. Whether in regard to the spiritual anticipation during Advent, or the childlike longing for Christmas Day to dawn with presents, the practice of hope in December is thoroughly ingrained into our culture. Of course, the idea of Christmas hope began more than 2,000 years ago, when Jesus was born in a lowly stable in Bethlehem. His coming was the fulfillment of hundreds of prophecies spoken by believers who had set their hope on the Savior who would finally rescue humanity from sin and death.

That same hope still exists today as we all eagerly wait for Jesus to return. It is so easy to unintentionally place our hope in people, things, or accomplishments that were never meant to bring us salvation. Instead, our only source of hope should be in Jesus, and Christmas offers a perfect opportunity to be reminded of this truth.

As you design your home this winter season, make sure it is filled with sights and sounds that communicate the true reason for the season. Whether through pictures, poems, paintings, or playlists, let hope fill your home and your heart so that it over-flows into the world around you.

Reimagine

What Christmas songs bring
you the most hope?

How do you like to incorporate music
into your home during Christmas?

What are some creative ways you can
share the message of hope in your home?

Scents of the Season

Welcoming Aromas

Scents and aromas can make or break a home—not only for guests but also for you! Do you have certain scents you gravitate toward? What aromas ease you into a happy, calm, cozy, or nostalgic mood? Are there certain smells you try to avoid, either due to preference, negative associations, or allergies? Check out some of the scent options below and see if you can freshen up the atmosphere of your home through aromas!

- Avoid room sprays or air fresheners that aren't natural.
- Bake cookies, bread, or other sweet-smelling treats.
- Create home potpourri in a simmer pot on the stove (use citrus, cranberries, spices like cinnamon or cloves, herbs, flowers, or other natural ingredients).
- Crush fresh lavender or sage.
- Light a candle (try to use natural candles made from beeswax).
- Run a diffuser with essential oils.
- Use more subtle or natural scents like lavender and eucalyptus.

SOCIALS

Family

And stretching out his hand toward his disciples, he said, "Here are my mother and my brothers! For whoever does the will of my Father in heaven is my brother and sister and mother."

—MATTHEW 12:49–50 (ESV)

CHRISTMAS SHOULD BE one of the most wonderful times of the year. After all, what's not to love about home-cooked meals, family traditions, lights in a tree, presents wrapped in bright ribbons, and stockings hung on a festive mantel? For many of us, Christmas means going "home for the holidays" and visiting family and friends we may not have seen since the year before. These final days in December let us take a much-needed respite and come together before the start of a brand-new year.

However, many of us experience Christmas as a season of loss or as a painful reminder of the family we wish we had. We might find the holidays challenging as we attempt to navigate difficult relationships with the family we do have. Still more of us have to face December 25 alone due to distance from loved ones or to inconvenient work schedules. Whatever the situation, Christmas may not be "wonderful" and the connection between "family" and "the holidays" may be strained. But there is hope.

As we read in Matthew, "family" should be a relative term for believers. In the capital "C" Church—the global body of believers—we are all part of the family of God, no matter what we may look like, what we might believe about real trees versus fake trees, or when we may start listening to Christmas music. Jesus calls us to be a light to the world, to feed those who are hungry, and to care for our neighbors. Though these callings are true for us throughout the year, we should be especially mindful of them during the season of hope and giving.

This Christmas, take a look at your home and evaluate the proportion between "you" space and "others" space. Is your home a place where neighbors can feel welcomed and loved?

Reimagine

Who could you welcome
into your family
this Christmas season?

How can your home be a haven
to those who are unable to spend
Christmas with their family?

How can your Christmas traditions
leave space for inviting and including
those around you?

Christmas Eve Brunch

Family and Food

To celebrate the idea of the spiritual family during the Christmas season, our family hosts a Christmas Eve brunch. We invite those who may not have biological family nearby but who are certainly spiritual family to us. As you can imagine, this annual brunch has become our favorite gathering of the season. Do you have special events that have become part of your Christmas tradition, either with friends or family? Are there certain dishes or activities that always must be included?

As you prepare your brunch or celebration, remember not to worry too much about the menu or the activities, since simply being together is the most rewarding thing you can do.

Tips for a Holiday Brunch

- Choose a color scheme.
- Create a Christmas playlist.
- Empty your dishwasher beforehand so it's ready to be loaded.
- Prepare some dishes ahead of time so you can just pop them in the oven.
- Set up one large table or several small tables.
- Stock up on to-go containers so you can send your guests home with leftovers.

Brunch Menu Ideas

- baked honey ham
- butternut squash soup
- chocolate pie
- cranberry-apple cobbler
- creamed potatoes or sweet potato casserole
- dinner rolls or monkey bread
- fresh green salad with sliced almonds, mandarin oranges, and pomegranates
- gingerbread or pumpkin loaf
- green bean casserole
- pumpkin macaroni and cheese

After-Brunch Ideas

- Build gingerbread houses.
- Decorate cookies.
- Make a Christmas craft.
- Play board games.
- Sing Christmas-carol karaoke.
- Watch a holiday movie.

About the Author and Photographer

SARABETH GALIMBA is a wife, mother of four, artist, interior decorator, real estate agent, and former youth pastor. She wrote her first book, *Reimagine Home,* as a personal and practical guide for those who want to bring simple beauty back into the look and life of their homes. When she is not working on a home project with her husband or trying out a new recipe, she enjoys spending time making memories with her family and sharing home styling tips through her Instagram account @ladyofthehome. She and her family live in the house featured in this book in Salinas, California, with their dog and pet chickens.